Thomas William Marshall

Order and chaos

a lecture, delivered at Loyola college, Baltimore, in July, 1869

Thomas William Marshall

Order and chaos

a lecture, delivered at Loyola college, Baltimore, in July, 1869

ISBN/EAN: 9783741193170

Manufactured in Europe, USA, Canada, Australia, Japa

Cover: Foto ©Thomas Meinert / pixelio.de

Manufactured and distributed by brebook publishing software
(www.brebook.com)

Thomas William Marshall

Order and chaos

ORDER AND CHAOS.

LADIES AND GENTLEMEN:

There is in our world a certain creation of human art, which some Christians are able to contemplate with sympathy and satisfaction; others, only with repugnance and disgust. You are all familiar with it, yet I do not flatter myself that I can describe it to you in a single sentence. It is too eccentric in its outward form, as well as too irregular in its internal structure, to be defined in a few words. No two fragments of this composite fabric, of which I am going to speak to you to-night, have the same shape, nor even belong to the same material. Perhaps the truest description of it would resemble that which the prophet gave of the "*great statue*" which the King of Babylon saw in his dream. Like that, it has "feet of clay," but it has also a head of wood, and a face of brass. All the wide regions of Chaos seem to have been searched, that they might contribute something towards its heterogeneous mass. Innumerable quarries have been opened, with a perverse industry, only to borrow from each a solitary specimen of its contents, so that nothing might be wanting to its perfection as a symbol of Disorder. With the materials thus derived, were built up, about three centuries ago, a new Tower of Babel. More successful than their ancestors in the plain of Sennaar, they were allowed to complete it. It has changed its original form many times since then, and is now almost without shape. It has fallen in here, and bulged out there, but though rent and torn in every direction, and only sustained by props and but-

5

tresses as decrepit as itself, it still stands, to the great astonishment even of its admirers, who predict every day that the final catastrophe is at hand. Around this falling Tower, you may see on certain days a confused multitude, who appear to meet together for a common purpose, but of whom it is to be noted that each individual speaks a different language, which no one can interpret, not even himself. The ear is wounded and bruised with the uproar of contending voices, which fill the air with ceaseless clamor, as if each strove to prevail over every other. The president of this tumultuous assembly is the Angel of Discord, and the building round which it is gathered is the Temple of Chaos. Yet there are men of excellent natural gifts, some even of great natural virtues, who have persuaded themselves to believe, and really do believe, that the architect of this monstrous fabric is the Most High God. They even imagine, so strong is their delusion, that the incoherent sounds which are heard in this temple constitute a species of worship peculiarly acceptable to Him, and much superior to anything of that kind hitherto invented by His creatures. But this curious fact need not surprise you, when you call to mind that the noblest intellects of antiquity — a Plato, a Socrates, or a Cicero — were able to accept as realities even the picturesque fictions of Pagan mythology; that an Alexander the Great, could seriously invoke Mercury, and a Julius Cæsar offer sacrifice to Minerva. Man is the same in every age, when left to himself, or to teachers like himself. In that lamentable condition, he can believe *anything* — except the truth. You know, ladies and gentlemen, what name has been given in every land to this Temple of Chaos. It has the same name in America as in Europe. Men call it Protestantism.

There is also in our world another creation, *not* of
human art, nor imitable by human skill. All the pre-
tended spiritual architects who ever lived, from Confu-
cius to Calvin, could not have fashioned *this* building,
nor any part of it. They could not even have imag-
ined it. From its foundation stone, which shall never
be moved, to its topmost pinnacles, which are reared
so high above the clouds that they are bathed day and
night in the pure light of Heaven, all is the work of
God. Man could no more make such a fabric as this
than he could make a world. It is the last and most
perfect conception of Omnipotent wisdom. It is the
mirror in which the Uncreated Beauty is most clearly
reflected. Within its walls only *one* language is spoken
and all can interpret it. It is the home of tranquil
peace, unbroken unity, and the largest liberty which
the creature can ever know. Long ages ago, the pro-
phets of Judah saw, in a vision, the building of which
I am now speaking, and even that far-off contempla-
tion of its glories filled them with rapture. *"Go round
about her,"* said one of them in a spirit of inspiration,
"mark well her towers; set your hearts on her strength."
" I will lay thy foundations with sapphires," cried another
in the same spirit, *"and I will make thy bulwarks of
jaspar, and thy gates of graven stones, ... and
great shall be the peace of thy children."* And lest men
should suppose that it was a thing of purely material
beauty, which they were invited only to *admire*, and
not a Living Power, which they were commanded to
obey, on pain of eternal death, the great prophet of Re-
demption uttered this final warning: *" The nation and
kingdom that will not serve thee shall perish, . . . No
weapon that is formed against thee shall prosper, and every
tongue that resisteth thee in judgment thou shalt condemn."*
And when at last the hour arrived, more than eighteen

centuries ago, when this " City of the Great King " was to be set up on earth, that its courts might be filled with human guests; when the same Omnipotent Voice which had once said, "*Let there be light*," now pronounced the new decree, "*Upon this rock I will build My church;*" it sprang at once into being, so perfect in its supernatural loveliness that even its Creator was enamoured of it, and called it His *Bride*. Never since He began to create had He given such a name to any thing which He had made. Never had He deigned to unite to Himself by such a tie any of His works. And as if all the magnificent promises which had gone before too feebly shadowed forth the glory to which this Bride was destined, He now added, no longer by the mouth of angel or prophet, but with His own lips, these astonishing words: "*The gates of hell shall not prevail against thee;*" and He confirmed the new promise by this transporting assurance: " *Behold, I am with thee all days, even to the consummation of the world.*" Other works which He had made might be defaced or come to an end, but not this, for He would keep it always in the hollow of His hand. Like the Temple of Chaos, of which I spoke just now, this building has also a name, a name known in heaven and on earth, and which, to us who dwell within its walls, is as music in the ear. Men call it the Catholic Church.

I presume to invite you this evening to visit these two buildings—the one human, and betraying in every stone its human origin; the other divine, and reflecting everywhere the beauty and majesty of Him who made it; the one, the Temple of Confusion and Chaos, and the prolific source of the worst evils which afflict human society; the other, the sole fountain of supernatural Order, both in the spiritual and the social sphere. But before we enter either of these temples, I ask your permission to make a single preliminary observation, which is necessary to prepare the way for the argument which I am going to address to you. It is this:

If there be in this lower world any authority which represents God, and speaks in His name—as all Christian communities, though with hesitating and stammering lips, profess to do, in some sense or other—that authority or institution, whatever it be, must reflect, as far as the creature can, the mind and the attributes of God. Otherwise it is convicted of imposture. For whatever in our world does *not* reflect God, in its own measure and proportion, is either a delusion or an abomination. Generally it is both at once. The whole argument which I am going to submit to your patient attention is based on this simple proposition. And now, keeping carefully in mind that whatever professes to belong to God must faithfully reflect Him, we may ask, without further preface, the question which this lecture is designed to answer: Is it in Protestantism, or in the Catholic Church, that the Divine presence and attributes are reflected?

I commence the reply to this question as follows. If we have any sure and rational conviction about God, it is this, that He is eternal *harmony*, essential *unity*, inviolable *order*, and ineffable *repose.* Even reason can find out thus much, as St. Paul reminded the heathen to their condemnation, by simply contemplating the visible universe. Is it, then, once more, in Protestantism, or in the Catholic Church, that harmony, unity, order, and repose are found? Let us visit the temple in which each dwells, and as courtesy requires us to give our first attention to strangers, let us begin with the Temple of Chaos. Our visit, I hasten to assure you, will be a brief one, and we may hope, in spite of its precarious condition, that it will not fall down whilst we are within it. 2

Well, I suppose that we have passed the portal of
this singular temple, and are fairly inside. What do
we see? Our first impression, which will be corrected
presently, is, that we have found our way into an empty
sepulchre. How chill and gloomy it is! It reminds
one of nothing so much as one of those Egyptian
tombs, monuments of the inanity of human pride,-
which people visit listlessly, as they visit other historical buildings, only to remark how perfectly useless
they have become. They note the broken tomb, or examine the empty sarcophagus, but hardly care to ask
whose dust it once contained. What is it to them?
But a greater surprise awaits us in this building. It
is supposed to be devoted to some kind of religious
worship, yet you cannot find in it, however long you
may remain, the faintest trace of God! Before we go
any further, let me offer you an explanation of His
absence. The founders of this structure, half-temple
and half-tomb, were in such a hurry to banish God
from it, in order to enthrone man in His place, that
they did not even pause to say, "Depart from us, O
Lord!" They were bringing in a new worship, in
which, as the event has proved, *man* was to be everything. Henceforth, the highest conception of religion
was to be — a group of men listening to a *man*. Yes,
they had brought Christianity to that. Every mystery
was now rejected. Mysteries, of which science could
give no account, might be tolerated in everything else,
because they could not get rid of them. There might
be mysteries all around them, and in their own persons, but at all events there should be none in religion.
And so they made short work of them. St. Paul had
said, *habemus altare,— we have an altar;* but the first act
of these new builders was to cry out: "*We* have neither
altar, nor priest, nor sacrifice." The next was to cast

the Christian altar to the ground. The tabernacle, in which God had dwelt for fifteen centuries, was broken to atoms. By these prompt and energetic proceedings they had already reduced the sacrifice of Mount Calvary to the dimensions of an historical event, of which henceforth no daily commemoration need be made. And the sequel was in harmony with this beginning. So eager were they to root out the very memory of the "*Daily Sacrifice*," which had been the chief rite and central mystery of the Christian religion, from the hearts of the people, and to substitute for it what the prophet Daniel, who foresaw this sacrilege, called "*the abomination of desolation*," i. e. the unprofitable talk of human teachers, that their leaders commanded the very altar stones to be placed in the porch, that all who came in might trample them under foot. This horrible iniquity, feebly imitated in later times by the Pagans of China and Japan, was actually enjoined by the English Ridley and his fellows, the founders of the Anglican church, and diligently accomplished throughout the realm of England. Can you wonder if from that hour God deserted the place? How should He dwell *there*, when they had taken His altars away? There was no longer any throne for Him. And so the place became, as His prophet foretold, "the abomination of desolation." The preacher is there, but not God. Man has taken His place.

But we are still only at the threshold of this deserted temple. As you stand there, it seems to you not only dark but empty. Yet you will find, as your eyes become accustomed to the feeble light, that it is not so. Advance a little into the interior, and you will see a curious scene. The whole place is filled with different groups, more than the eye can count, and in the midst of each is a man, who is addressing those around him.

If your ear could take in simultaneously what each speaker says, you would find that they are all talking about the same thing, and all giving a different account of it. Every man is flatly contradicting in his own group what is being confidently asserted in the group next to him. And many of the hearers constantly pass to and fro from one to the other, and seem to be equally pleased with the affirmation and the contradiction. Some have not made up their minds which to prefer. But as it is impossible to hear them all at once, and would be intolerable to hear them all in succession, I propose to you that we should select one of the groups at random, and join ourselves to it. There is a man in the middle of it, as in all the others. He occupies a sort of pulpit, and seems to be preaching. But he is not. He is praying, only he does it after a fashion of his own, with which you are not familiar. I must attempt to describe it to you. He knows very well that the people there are listening to him, and that he is expected to be what they call "impressive;" so he proceeds to satisfy the expectation to the best of his ability. You may often read in certain newspapers, having a large circulation in the regions of Chaos, of certain religious ceremonies, in which one of the officiating personages is invariably reported to have offered "an impressive prayer." I have read such an announcement a hundred times. You will ask, perhaps, how in the world can a man on his knees before the dread majesty of God contrive to be "impressive?" The notion of trying to produce a *sensation* under such circumstances seems to you as wildly extravagant as if a man should undertake to sing a comic song at his own funeral. But you are not acquainted with the resources of a ministerial artist in the Temple of Chaos. He can do things quite as difficult as this. Of course,

he can only do it in one way,—by forgetting all about
God, and thinking only of himself, and the poor creatures around him. In this way, he can be, after a
certain fashion, very impressive indeed—at least in his
own judgment and theirs. But the misfortune is that
his hearers, who also forget all about God, are tempted
to worship the preacher instead, who has not much
objection to their doing so, and is still more irresistibly
tempted to worship himself. You and I only know of
two kinds of prayer, one offered in heaven, the other
on earth, and neither of them in the least resembles the
style of prayer which is known in the Temple of Chaos.
In heaven, the mightiest angels, at the bare sight of
whom the strongest among ourselves would faint away
with fear, cover their faces with their wings, and hardly
dare to look up: on earth, they who will one day con-
sort with angels, also hide their faces, smite their
breasts, and say, "God be merciful to me a sinner."
They both see a Vision before them which takes away
all ambition of being "impressive." *They* are not
thinking of themselves, but of Him in whose presence
they stand. How should they turn away their eyes to
any meaner object? We are told indeed of a certain
Pharisee, who "prayed *within himself*," a phrase of
which you have often appreciated the significance,—
and he too, I doubt not, was very impressive to those
who happened to be looking at him. But you remember what our Lord, who was also looking at him, said
of his prayer.

In spite of this formidable judgment, I venture to
predict that, if you are in the habit of looking at the
public journals, you will read, before a week has
elapsed, of somebody offering somewhere, an "impressive" prayer. There is a class of teachers with whom
it is a professional necessity to do so. They are paid

to be impressive, and cannot escape the miserable obligation. It is a melancholy fact that, in too many cases, their prayers are offered, not to God, who does not require them to be impressive, but to *man* who insists upon their being so, and would consider himself defrauded, if they were not. This is one of the fatal consequences of putting man in the place of God. In the sight of God, we are only impressive when we forget *ourselves;* in the sight of man, we have most claim to admiration when we forget *Him*. And thus it comes to pass that, in the Temple of Chaos, what professes to be a supplication to God, is really a discourse to men, and what might have been a good prayer, is converted into a bad sermon.

However, the gentleman with whom we are immediately concerned, has finished his eloquent prayer, and is now beginning to preach. Let us hear what he has got to say. We have come into his temple at a fortunate moment, for he is preaching about heaven. But as you listen, you will find that it is not the heaven to which *you* aspire—the heaven of saints and martyrs. He has nothing to tell us about that, probably because he knows nothing about it. He is immensely affecting about what he calls "the recognition of departed friends," and "the reunion of husbands and wives,"—as if the chief employment in heaven was to be the perpetual celebration of nuptial rites,—and he draws such a ravishing picture of these human delights, he is so steeped and saturated in earthly anticipations, that we are almost tempted to think the man must be a Mahometan. His hearers, who are evidently enchanted, do not seem to care much whether he is or not, and the earthly view of heaven which he advocates with so much pathos seems to be sufficiently attractive to them. They do not appear to notice, as you and I do, that in his enumeration of future joys, he does not make the slightest allusion to God, and perhaps they think, if they think about it at all, that it is quite consistent, after banishing Him from *their* temple on earth, that they should expel Him from His own temple in heaven. With their peculiar views of celestial felicity, which is simply the perpetuation of familiar joys and the society of sympathising friends, heaven would probably be a much more agreeable residence without Him. I fear it must be said that the Beatific Vision, if they had ever heard of it, would rather repel than attract them. They consider too that heaven belongs to them,—one does not exactly understand by what title,—and as they fortunately possess the power to admit all their friends, without whom it might be a little dull and monotonous, it is natural that they should be generous, and to borrow a phrase of this world, " keep open house." Perhaps, they sometimes abuse the privilege. I have heard since I came here of a book, which I have not seen, but which is described, by those who have, as a meritorious attempt to be witty, without the smallest success. It is called, I am told, " the Comedy of Canonization." I can say nothing about its contents, of which I am wholly ignorant, but I very much approve its title. It *is* a transparent Comedy, that people who belong to the same school as the writer of this book, and who disdain the slow and cautious judicial proceedings of the Roman courts, should canonize all *their* friends, whatever may have been the nature of their life or opinions, and without a syllable of enquiry, as soon as the breath is out of their bodies. I agree with the Baltimore clergyman that this *is* a very comic proceeding indeed, only I am not quite sure that these jubilant decrees of canonization pronounced in the Temple of Chaos are always ratified in the

Temple of God. But we are forgetting our preacner, who by this time has almost got to the end of his sermon. I confess to a suspicion, begotten in my mind while listening to him, that the only rapturous feeling with which *he* anticipates Paradise, is inspired by the delightful expectation that he will there find a congregation who will never go to sleep, and to whom he may preach for all eternity. This, I suspect, is his private notion of celestial bliss. Let us hope, for the sake of his congregation, that he will be disappointed. It is dreary enough, judging by this specimen, to listen to one such sermon: who can conceive a more terrible fate than to have to listen to it for ever? An official of the great University of Oxford, once observed to a visitor, to whom he was showing the beauties of that ancient city; " I have heard all the sermons preached in the University pulpit for forty years, and thank God, Sir, I am still able to believe in the truth of christianity." I suppose that most persons whose hard fate it has been to hear such sermons, in which the vanity of one man makes such an exorbitant demand upon the patience of many, would confess that they rarely come to the close of life without a feeling of bitter resentment against those who had inflicted so heavy a trial upon them. I conceive too that if the epitaph of most of the preachers in the Temple of Chaos were composed, not by the heirs of their worldly goods, who can afford to offer them a parting compliment which costs nothing, but by their more dispassionate hearers, it would be apt to resemble that which was suggested for the tomb of a well known architect, who had covered the earth with many a pile, not of words but of bricks, and over whose body it was proposed to inscribe these vindictive lines :

"Lie heavy on him, Earth, for he
Laid many a heavy load on thee."

But it is the peculiar misfortune of all the worshipers in the Temple of Chaos that, let the preacher be ever so flat, stale and unprofitable, let his dull conceit impel him to handle subjects ever so far above his comprehension, *they* have no alternative but patience—unless they prefer slumber. One shudders to think of the sufferings inflicted, especially upon innocent women and children, by the insatiable vanity of human preachers, " these earthly god-fathers of heaven's lights," as Shakspeare calls them. The late Sydney Smith, who could say bitter things, as some of you know, about those who offended him, and who said very bitter things indeed about certain people in Pennsylvania, once suggested, I suppose after being irritated by a tedious sermon, that it would be a righteous retribution if the man himself could be " preached to death by wild curates." The famous Canon of St. Paul's must have been very angry when he uttered this intemperate wish, for only the extremest ferocity of malice could desire to condemn a fellow-creature to such a fate. It may be, however, that a better day is in store for these poor sufferers, who begin to find that they have not gained much by putting God out of their temples, and substituting man in his place. Man-worship has proved to be a dreary as well as an unprofitable amusement. Already, murmurs deep and loud are heard. English newspapers and reviews—I do not know how it is in this country—are full of indignant protestations against the prosy incapacity or feeble sensationalism of self-complacent preachers, and perhaps their reign is drawing to a close. I once heard the sorrowful indignation of their victims expressed in such ingenious terms, that I will venture to relate the anecdote to you. " How hard it is," said a Protestant, whom I knew and loved, " that we can never go to Church without being forced

3

to listen to a bad essay, in which there is nothing amusing except the vanity of the preacher." "Every age," responded another, whose name is known to you if I were at liberty to mention it, "has its own peculiar trials. Thus, the primitive Christians suffered martyrdom, and *we* suffer—sermons." I am happy to add that both these gentlemen have since become Catholics, and are now acquainted with an order of preachers who speak only of divine things, and who are too much absorbed in striving to promote the glory of God, to have much leisure to think about their own.

And now, ladies and gentlemen, as we shall certainly gain nothing by prolonging our visit, we will quit the Temple of Chaos. I know not whether you have remarked it, but to me it seems there is a smell of earth in it which after a few minutes becomes overpowering. However long we staid there, we should find always the same dismal entertainment—a man talking to men. That is the beginning and end of it. The human can only beget the human. Let us go out into the pure air, where we can breathe more freely, and where we can make certain reflections which our visit suggests. But before we do so, let us enter for a moment that other temple with which we are more familiar, and where a different scene awaits us.

Do not fear that I am going to describe to you what you all know so well. I will ask you to notice only a single point of contrast in the two buildings. In the one which we have just quitted, man is the sole object of attraction; in that which we now enter, man is nothing, and God everything. There are indeed human ministers in this temple also, to whom we give our love, our gratitude, and our respect, and none know better than you how well they deserve them; but they will be the first to approve my words when I say, that it is not *their*

presence which attracts us. We go as gladly, drawn
by the same irresistible power, when they are absent,
as when they are present. I will not say we can do
without them, which would be senseless ingratitude,
for they are "the stewards of the mysteries of God,"
and have been endowed with special gifts for our sake;
but this I will say, and you will confirm it, that even
when they stand before the altar, neither do they think
of us, nor we of them, except to recommend each other
to the same Master, whose Presence makes both them
and us forget every other. This is the essential difference between the two temples, of which, the one is all
human, the other all Divine. It has often been admitted, at least in part, even by those who could discern the contrast without deriving any lesson from it.
The present Duke of Argyle, who is a sort of Presbyterian, has confessed, in one of his writings, probably
because he thought it useless to deny it, that within the
precincts of the Temple of Chaos, man is everything,
and that people only go to church for the sake of the
preacher. I will only add that the two modes of worship display in every other detail all the difference
which might be expected between what is human and
what is Divine. Consider if this be not so. There is
in the whole Book of Revelation only one description
of the worship in heaven. What is it? It is such an
exact description of the worship which you may see
any day in any Catholic Church of this city, that only
inveterate and judicial blindness can hinder men from
seeing that the one is a mirror in which the other is
reflected. See how exactly the rites correspond. In
heaven, we are told, by one who saw what he describes,
there is an "altar," and upon the altar "a lamb that
was slain," and on their knees before this altar wor-
shipping spirits, who offer "incense" from "golden

censers," and make intercession for their brethren on earth. That is St. John's description. Who does not see that nothing which is done on earth resembles it except the Holy Mass? You know, on the other hand, what sort of worship they offer in the Temple of Chaos. We looked in just now for a moment to see it. There was a man talking, but there was neither altar, nor victim, nor silent adorers, nor golden censers, nor the sweet perfume of incense, nor the intercession of saints. There was literally *nothing* of what the apostle describes. Compare this naked human scene, repulsive in its earthliness, with what takes place in the Sanctuary which *you* frequent, and say, which seems to you the truest resemblance of the worship which St. John saw in heaven?

If, then, in considering the question whether God and His attributes are most clearly reflected in the Temple of Chaos or in the Catholic Church, we limit our enquiry to the two buildings, and to what goes on within them, the decision cannot be doubtful. We may even say, that if it were possible to regard the skeleton ritual of the human sects — in which the only pretence of *unity* consists in a common resolve to suppress the truth, the only attempt at *variety* in the multitude of errors substituted for it — as a counterpart, however remote, of heaven, men would no longer expect the future life with eager desire, but with unutterable dismay. No one, in truth, not even, I suppose, our Protestant friends, would desire to dwell in *such* a heaven. The angels would abandon it with horror. Yet there is not one of *you* who does not know, by a most blissful experience, that the worship in every *Catholic* church is a true and real reflection of that which is offered round the throne of God; that the joy with which it inspires you is the same in kind, though not in degree, as that which you will hereafter derive from the Beatific Vision; and finally, that it is no exaggeration, but the simple truth, to say, that whenever you assist at the sublime mystery of the Christian altar, in which God offers Himself to God,* and take part in that august worship which alone is equal in worth and majesty to Him who is worshipped; for *you* the true life of Paradise has already begun, and *you* can aspire to the joy which God has prepared for you in the Church in heaven, because you have already tasted that kindred joy which He gives you in the Church on earth.

Thus far we have noticed only a single point of the contrast between the kingdoms of Order and of Chaos. We have insisted, not without reason, that a religion which reflects nothing in heaven can only be the product of earth—unless you trace its origin to a still lower region. We may now advance a step in our argument, and proceed to prove, if indeed it needs to be proved, that a religious system which is the most complete negation to be found among men of all the prime attributes of God, and especially of the Divine *Order* and *Unity*, cannot have God for its author, because God cannot contradict Himself.

I suppose I may venture to assert, without fear of contradiction from any quarter, that if there is anything absolutely repugnant to the nature of God, it is Confusion and Disorder. Sin itself is not more abhorrent to Him than the Disorder which is but the fruit and evidence of sin. Examine the material creation, and find, if you can, a single department of it which is not under the inexorable reign of *Law*. From the stately march of the planets in their orbit to the insect in the narrow home in which every want of its ephe-

* *Ipse offerens, Ipse et oblatio.—St. Augustine.*

meral life is provided, in every corner of the Universe,
and in every form of matter, animate or inanimate,
Law and Order assert their despotic and uncontested
dominion. Even the king of poets understates the
truth, when he says:

> "There is nothing, situate under heaven's eye,
> But hath his bound, in earth, and sea, and sky."

I am not going to weary you with many examples,
but you will permit me to notice one or two, which will
render any further illustration of this point superflu-
ous. If you find, as you certainly will, that even where
Order is least apparent — nay, that even in the very
phenomena which seem to be the direct result of its
absence — an energetic and invariable law is actively
working; you will feel that this part of our case is
superabundantly proved. I will give you only three
examples, to which I solicit your patient attention,—
one in the far-off regions of space, one on the earth,
and·one in the clouds which are its curtain and canopy.

1. When the great Kepler strove to penetrate the
mystery of our planetary system, and to correct the
astronomical errors of the Egyptian Ptolemy, he was
startled by this discovery. He found that the various
planets which revolve in that system appeared, at a
first glance, to have been formed and projected into
space, without order or method. They all varied in
dimension, in density, in velocity, and in their distance
from the sun. In the smaller planets, or asteroids, as
Vesta and Pallas, a man could spring into the air sixty
feet, and return to the ground without a shock; while
in other planets his own weight would crush him to
atoms, so great is the force of attraction. In a word,
they differed in every point, and seemed to have no
mutual relation. Here, then, was a singular apparent

absence of law and order. When Kepler saw this, inspired partly by his genius änd partly by a profound religious sentiment, he said to himself: "That is not so! There *is* a law, if I could only find it, for God is never at variance with Himself." And then, after many a patient toil and vigil, he made that splendid discovery which astronomers call the Third Law of Kepler. Not only did he find a law even in this apparent confusion, but a law which could be expressed with mathematical precision, which bound together in a magnificent symmetry every planet in our system, and which disclosed to him and to us this truth—that the squares of their periodic times are proportioned to the cubes of their mean distances from the sun. It was then that the illustrious student, full of gratitude to Him from whom all knowledge comes, cried out, with a rapture which was more religious than scientific: " I have stolen the golden vases of the Egyptians, to build up a tabernacle for my God."

2. The second example which I will briefly notice is not less remarkable. The late Alexander Von Humboldt, who probably possessed as much human and as little divine knowledge as any man who ever lived, used to say that if the philosophers of an earlier generation had carefully observed the phenomena of terrestial magnetism, discoveries of the most momentous kind might have rewarded their labour. He probably did not know that, more than a century before any one else had paid much attention to the subject, the missionaries of the Society of Jesus, as great in human as in divine science, had been in the habit of constantly registering during their innumerable apostolic journeys, the variations of the magnetic currents. All honor to this noble Society, to which we all owe so much. But what I wish you to notice is a fact which later investigations

in this science have revealed, that even the most apparently eccentric movements of that subtle and mysterious agent to which I am alluding, and which heretofore were supposed to be due to purely accidental causes, are now known to be the result of an invariable *law;* so that in this department of creation also, and generally even in what are called the "disturbing forces" of nature, the idea of confusion is finally eliminated, and we learn once more that, in all the works of God, from the least to the greatest, when you rashly deem that you are face to face with Chaos, one ray of light dispels the mists which produced the deception, and Order stands unveiled before your astonished gaze.

3. One more illustration, and then I will endeavor to complete my argument, and release you from the attention which I am so little able to recompense. If there be anything in nature, anything of which man's senses can take cognizance, which appears to belong undeniably to the realm of Chaos, it is surely the tempest, which, on sea or land, bears ruin on its wings, leaves ruin in its track, and seems to have the same relation to Order, which Madness has to Reason. But we have learned by this time to distrust appearances, especially when we are talking about the works of the Creator. And what is the fact? Your own Maury has shown in this country, and Colonel Reid in England, that even the hurricane and the cyclone, in all their might and fury, are as docile to the reign of *law* as the humblest machine constructed by human ingenuity is submissive to the hand that made it, and the English writer referred to has actually given to his book this significant title, "The *Law* of Storm."

And now to apply these facts, and show how they bear upon our argument. You are asked to believe, by those who prefer the Temple of Chaos to the Sanctuary of God, this monstrous proposition; — that although Disorder is inexorably banished, as we have seen, from every other part of His dominions, as a thing abhorrent to the Divine Architect, it finds its true home and congenial refuge precisely in that spiritual kingdom of which He is at once the Law Giver and the Life. Brute matter knows nothing of it; earth, and sea, and sky, refuse to give it a place; the very beasts of the field obey a law which regulates all the conditions of their existence; but Confusion and Chaos, which can find a home nowhere else, reign, and ought to reign, in the Christian Church, and in the kingdom of souls! That is the proposition which is deliberately maintained, at this hour, and in this land, by men whose profession it is to teach others eternal truth. They gravely assert that Religion—which, when it is Divine, is a bond of union stronger than adamant, and when it is human, is the most active dissolvent, the most powerful disintegrating agent which divides and devastates modern society—*gains* by ceasing to be one, and that Christianity derives its chief vitality from the very divisions which make it contemptible in the sight of unbelievers, and had often provoked the scorn and derision even of the pagan world. As this statement may seem to you impossible, even in this nineteenth century, which is tolerant of all absurdities in the sphere of religion, I will quote to you the very words of one of the most conspicuous preachers of this land, who holds a high position in the Hierarchy of Chaos. I take them from one of your own local journals, of the second of this month, (June.) You know that of late years many Protestants, weary of their ceaseless conflicts and ashamed of their unending divisions, have begun at last to sigh for the unity which they have lost,

4

and that in England they have even formed a society, with the express object of bringing together what they ignorantly call "the different branches of the Church." We are told, however, by the journal to which I allude, that the Reverend Henry Ward Beecher, vehemently rejecting every such project, lately "preached against the schemes of church union, whether planned by Pope, Protestant, or Pagan,"—pray understand that these are not my words,—and added this characteristic dissuasive from unity. "The strength of the Christian religion lies," he said,—in what do you suppose? in its truth, its holiness, or its peace? no, but—"*in the number of the existing denominations.*" The hands fall down in reading such·words. "I pray," said He who will judge the world, "that they may all be *one*, as Thou, Father, art in Me, and I in Thee." I sincerely trust, replies Mr. Beecher, that they never will be one. "Be perfect," said St. Paul, "in the *same mind* and the *same judgment.*" It is much more important, rejoins Mr. Beecher, that you should maintain your divisions and perpetuate your differences, for in *them* lies the strength of Christianity. "Sects," observed the same Apostle, "are the work of the flesh." Mr. Beecher judges them more leniently, and warns his hearers, as you see, against the mistake of St. Paul. Yes, these human teachers have come at last to this. They know so well that supernatural Unity is beyond *their* reach, that they have come to hate it, and to call it an evil! Yet even they will not deny that it was the Unity of the first Christians which conquered the heathen world; and when the victory was accomplished, and the surviving pagans had only strength enough left to beat themselves against the ground where they had fallen, *they* also cried out in their impotent rage: "*Execranda est ista consensio*—cursed be this Unity of the Christians."

They had found it to be invincible, but did not know that it was Divine. Mr. Beecher dares not say openly, "Cursed be the Unity for which Christ prayed," for even his disciples, though they can bear a good deal, could not bear *that;* but he is not afraid to say: "Blessed be Chaos!" "Confusion, thou art my choice!" "Disorder, be thou mine inheritance!" Let us wish him a happier lot, both in this world and the next.

The truth is that our separated friends do not and cannot understand the sacred mystery of Unity, because they are so exclusively occupied about man, that the secrets of God are hidden from them. What is Unity? It is in essence purely Divine, and in its perfection exists only in the Adorable and Incomprehensible Trinity. But for this very reason, whenever you find Unity in created things, you may be sure that you are looking upon an image and reflection of God. Now there is in this world one society, and one only, in which that Unity has never been interrupted. That society is at once the most numerous and the most ancient of all Christian communities. It is found in all Kingdoms and States, it reaches from pole to pole, and embraces all orders and degrees of men. Yet, in spite of the infinite diversity of their character and temperament, of their education, modes of thought, habits of life, sympathies, prejudicies, language, and of whatsoever else distinguishes man from man; this vast multitude, speaking all the dialects of the world, and differing from each other, often with unnecessary vehemence, about all else, are as indissolubly *one* in all which relates to supernatural truth,—to God, their own souls, and the relations between them,—as if they had only one heart and one mind. And they are *one*, not only in faith, but even in discipline and government. In the whole history of the human race there

is no record of any such miracle as this. If all the
dead should come to life again at the same hour, and
crowd our streets and thoroughfares, it would not be a
greater. The men of this generation, like the Jews of
old, "*desire a sign*," in order that they may believe.
Here is one more luminous than the noonday sun. The
lightning does not shine out of heaven with a more
dazzling brightness. The essential character of God
is *Unity*, and whatever professes to belong to Him,
whether in the kingdon of nature or of grace, must
reflect that Unity. If it does not, it is not His work.
Now, not only do the sects know nothing of it, but
their very existence is a perpetual protest against it.
Yet in the Church, though her children are, by nature,
frail and mutable, like all the children of Adam, there
is a Unity and a Repose like the Unity and the Repose of God. Who has wrought this marvel? Consider over what an array of countless impossibilities
this miraculous Unity of the Church has triumphed.
The supple Italian, keen of wit and of ardent imagination; the stolid Englishman, who moves slowly to
attain his ends, but only to pursue them with a more
unwearied tenacity; the brilliant Frenchman, who
unites restless vivacity with exquisite common sense,
and is not more fertile in inventing paradox than
merciless in exposing it; the thoughtful German, who
numbers all the truths in his possession like objects in
a museum, and knows exactly the place which he has
assigned to each; the stately Spaniard, who is almost
oriental in his immobility, and in whom we discern a
gravity of mind which gives even to the mendicant the
dignity of a king; the impulsive Irishman, who has
more wit than the English, more enthusiasm than the
German, and, wherever he finds fair play and just laws,
more industry than either of them; the acute American,

whose boast it is that no difficulty can baffle his enterprise nor any counterfeit escape his detection; all these, and twenty other races whom I do not stay to enumerate, contrasting violently with each other in every natural gift and habit, while retaining all their distinctive peculiarities as men and citizens, become absolutely *one*, as if all fashioned in the same mould, and moved by the same spirit, as Christians and Catholics. And this astonishing unity of elements so various and contradictory is perpetuated from age to age, in a world where all else is in a state of chronic flux and solution, silently, peacefully, without effort, and without constraint. Nay, so irresistible is the mysterious power which works this miracle, that even the convert of yesterday, whether in the centres of European civilization or amid the semi-barbarous populations of China or Hindostan, though admitted but a few hours ago into the family of God, has already the sweet spell upon him, and finds, to his own exceeding astonishment, that his heart beats in unison with the great heart of the Church, as if he had been suckled at her breasts, and had lain in her bosom from infancy.

On the other hand, in the human communities which owe their existence to earthly founders, though there is much virtue, much acuteness, much learning, it has ever been found impossible to keep even the members of the same sect—I will not say in one country, or in one town, or in one village, but alas! in one family—from perpetual disputes even about the sublimest truths of revealed religion. Never since the Fall has the enemy, whose mission it is to scatter and divide, obtained so great a triumph over any portion of our race—a triumph so complete, that even the same individual at different epochs of his life, is often in flagrant contradiction with himself, avows to-day opinions which yesterday he abhorred, and which to-morrow he will exchange once more for new ones, and after belonging successively to various religious denominations, frequently ends by professing equal contempt for them all. And thus it has come to pass that in the world of Chaos,—in that dismal region which lies outside the Church of God,—two modes of thought now prevail to the gradual exclusion of all others: the first, that truth is what every man thinks it to be; the second, which is the logical equivalent of the first, that truth has no existence.

In presence of this immense contrast, which the least observant of mankind can detect, between the indefectible unity of the Church and the hopeless disorder of the sects, the members of the latter have felt the urgent necessity of attempting some explanation. They have comprehended, in spite of the inactivity of their spiritual apprehension, that since Unity is an infallible indication of the presence of God, *because God alone can produce it*, it follows that it is only in the Catholic Church that He resides. The conclusion is peremptory, and they feel it to be so. For this reason, while some have ventured in their anger to revile Unity, which is to blaspheme God, and to sing the praises of Disorder, which is to chant a hymn to Satan; others have sought to *account* for the Unity which they despair of attaining on purely human grounds. It is, they say, the subtle organization, the persevering arts, and the inexplicable skill of the Roman Church which binds all her members together with that adamantine chain which neither the world nor the devil can break asunder. They do not seem to perceive that the answer is suicidal, like that which the serpent makes when he turns his fangs against himself, and dies of his own sting. Catholic Unity the result of human art! Why the same men tell us every day, with the touching humility and self-abasement which, as you know, is the chief characteristic of Protestantism, that sagacity, enlightenment, penetration, knowledge of the human heart, skilful diagnosis, and generally every mental and spiritual pre-eminence, are their own peculiar heritage; while *we* are so slenderly equipped with both moral and intellectual gifts, that our continued success in attracting the pure, the wise, and the learned of all ages and countries is the most incomprehensible of the triumphs of the Catholic Church. If, then, Catholic Unity be the result of *human* art, will these spiritual and intellectual giants tell us how it is that *they* are totally unable to imitate it? What! so much more ingenious and spiritual than we are, and yet always ignominiously baffled in doing what the Church always accomplishes without effort? There is evidently nothing serious in such an explanation as this. It means nothing, and was not intended to mean anything. What, then, is this Power which is given to us, and denied to them? If it be human, let them define and localize it. But this they will never do. They cannot say *where* nor *what* it is, because its source is concealed in a far-off region to which *they* have no access. The earth says, It is not in me. The sea murmurs, It is not in me. Hell confesses, It is not in me. If, then, by the testimony of all mankind, there is one Power, and one only, which works this miracle, and unites all hearts in a mysterious and supernatural unity, in spite of human frailty and caprice, and if that Power can be found neither on the earth nor under the earth, where shall we look for it but in heaven?

We are sometimes told that good men abide contentedly in some earthly sect because, in spite of honest intentions, they are really unable to recognize the true

Church. It may be so, though such involuntary ignorance seems to us only a bare possibility. For if St. Paul could say, as he did, to the heathen world, "you might have found out the true God by His *works*, if you had cared to do so;" surely the God of St. Paul may say to the children of Chaos in the great Day, "you might have known the true Church by her *Unity*, if you had not closed your eyes."

Without presuming to anticipate the judgments of God, which we have neither the power nor the inclination to do, there is one conclusion which even we mortals can draw, without the risk of error, from the considerations which I have now submitted to you. We have seen that in the kingdom of souls, as in the kingdom of matter, it is the will of the Most High that His own essential Unity should be reflected. It follows, that religious sects, which are the perpetual negation of that Unity, can only be agreeable to Him on this supposition,—either that He has changed His nature, or that, having failed to suppress what is in irreconcileable opposition with Himself, He ceased to take any further interest in the affairs of men, and consented, as far as they were concerned, that Order should be replaced by Chaos.

It is to be noted of the argument which I have just employed, that while the most powerful intellect can suggest no reply to it, a little child can use it with full appreciation of its force. Permit me to give you a proof of this.

Some years ago, I was present officially at the examination of an English primary school, in which the children displayed such unusual accuracy and intelligence as long as the questions turned only upon secular subjects, that I was anxious to ascertain whether they could reason as well about the truths of the Catechism, as they could about those of Grammar and Arithmetic. I communicated my desire to their clergyman, who kindly permitted me to have recourse to a test which I had employed on other occasions. I requested him to interrogate them on the Notes of the Church, and when they had explained in the usual manner the meaning of the word Catholic, I took up the examination, with the consent of the Priest, and addressed the following question to the class: "You say the Church is Catholic because she is everywhere. Now, I have visited many countries, in all parts of the world, and I never came to one in which I did not find heresy. If, then, the Church is Catholic because she is everywhere, why is not heresy Catholic, since heresy is everywhere also?" "If you please, sir," answered a little girl about twelve years of age, "the Church is everywhere, and everywhere the *same;* heresy may be everywhere too, as you say, but it is everywhere *different.*"

I related this incident not long after, as a proof that faith is an intellectual power, to one of the greatest lawyers in England, a man accustomed to appraise all the products of the human intellect. He declared to me his opinion that it was the most astonishing answer ever made by a child. He was wrong. I have myself heard similar answers a hundred times. And you, Ladies and Gentlemen, will certainly not share the surprise of this eminent lawyer, because you know that a little Catholic child, who has learned the Catechism, and nothing else, is a truer and deeper philosopher, in the sight of God and the angels, than all the Pagan sages of the past, or all the Protestant doctors of the present.

As I have strayed once more into the region of anecdote, perhaps you will allow me to linger there for a

5

moment. It may relieve the tediousness of a discussion which I fear has exhausted your patience, if I add two or three which will be found to possess at least this merit, that they all confirm, in various ways, the argument which I have had the honour to address to you this evening.

A young English lady, with whom I became subsequently acquainted, and from whose lips I heard the tale, informed her parents that she felt constrained to embrace the Catholic faith. Hereupon arose much agitation in the parental councils, and a reluctant promise was extorted from the daughter that she would not communicate with any Catholic priest till she had first listened to the convincing arguments with which certain clerical friends of the family would easily dissipate her unreasonable doubts. These ministers were three in number, and we will call them Messrs. A, B, and C. The appointed day arrived for the solemn discussion, which one of the ministers was about to commence, when the young lady opened it abruptly with the following remark: "I am too young and uninstructed to dispute with gentlemen of your age and experience, but perhaps you will allow me to ask you a few questions?" Anticipating an easy triumph over the poor girl, the three ministers acceded with encouraging smiles to her request. "Then I will ask you," she said to Mr. A., "whether regeneration always accompanies the Sacrament of Baptism?" "Undoubtedly," was the prompt reply, "that is the plain doctrine of our Church." "And you, Mr. B.," she continued, "Do you teach that doctrine?" "God forbid, my young friend," was his indignant answer, "that I should teach such soul-destroying error. Baptism is a formal rite, which," &c., &c. "And you, Mr. C.," she asked the third, "what is your opinion?" "I regret," he replied with a bland voice, for he began to suspect they were making a mess of it, "that my reverend friends should have expressed themselves a little incautiously. The true doctrine lies between these extremes "—and he was going to develop it, when the young lady, rising from her chair, said : "I thank you, gentlemen, you have taught me all that I expected to learn from you. You are all ministers of the same Church, yet you each contradict the other even upon a doctrine which St. Paul calls one of the *foundations* of Christianity. You have only confirmed me in my resolution to enter a Church whose ministers all teach the same thing." And then they went out of the room one by one, and probably continued their battle in the street. But the parents of the young lady turned her out of doors the next day, to get her bread as she could. They sometimes do that sort of thing in England.

Another friend of mine, also a lady, and one of the most intelligent of her sex, was for several years the disciple of the distinguished minister who has given a name to a certain religious school in England. Becoming disaffected towards the Episcopalian Church, which appeared to her more redolent of earth in proportion as she aspired more ardently towards heaven, she was persuaded to assist at a certain Ritualistic festival, which it was hoped would have a soothing effect upon her mind. A new church was to be opened, and the ceremonies were to be prolonged through an entire week. All the Ritualistic celebrities of the day were expected to be present. Her lodging was judiciously provided in a house in which were five of the most transcendental members of the High Church party. It was hoped that they would speedily convince her of their apostolic unity, but unfortunately, they only succeeded in proving to her that no two of

them were of the same mind. One recommended her
privately to pray to the Blessed Virgin, which another
condemned as, at best, a poetical superstition. One
told her that the Pope was by Divine appointment the
head of the Universal Church; another, that he was a
usurper and a schismatic. One maintained that the
" Reformers" were profane scoundrels and apostates;
another, that they had at all events good intentions.
But I need not trouble you with an account of their
various creeds. Painfully affected by this diversity,
where she had been taught to expect complete uni-
formity, her doubts were naturally confirmed. During
the week she was invited to take a walk with the
eminent person whom she had hitherto regarded as a
trustworthy teacher. To him she revealed her growing
disquietude, and presumed to lament the conflict of
opinions which she had lately witnessed, but only to
be rewarded by a stern rebuke; for it is a singular fact
that men who are prepared at any moment to judge all
the Saints and Doctors, will not tolerate any judgment
which reflects upon themselves. It was midwinter, and
the lady's companion, pointing to the leafless trees by
the roadside, said, with appropriate solemnity of voice
and manner: "They are stripped of their foliage now,
but wait for the spring, and you will see them once
more wake to life. So shall it be with the Church of
England, which now seems to you dead." "It may be
so," she replied, " but what sort of a spring can we expect, *after a winter which has lasted three hundred years?*"
You will not be surprised to hear that this lady soon
after became a member of a Church which knows
nothing of winter, but within whose peaceful borders
reigns eternal spring.

My next anecdote, you will be glad to hear that it is
the last, shall be borrowed from your own country. A

few weeks ago, the heads of one of the largest religious
denominations of this land assembled in council. Their
body had been split into two sections, and they desired
to heal the schism. "It is *impossible* to do so," observed
one of them, who appears to have had some dim conception of the nature of Christian truth, "for we differ
on the gravest points of doctrine." But the majority
promptly overruled this trivial objection. What was
mere unity of doctrine compared with the advantage
of presenting an apparently united front to the public
eye? And so the objectors were silenced, as such objectors generally are in the Temple of Chaos. One gentleman, a Doctor of Divinity,—of what sort of Divinity
you will see in a moment,—clenched the whole matter
with this decisive argument: "We do not differ," he
said, "about doctrine, but only about the philosophy
of doctrine." From which ingenious distinction you
clearly perceive, that when one man teaches the Atone-
ment, and another denies it; or, when one believes in
the Incarnation, and the other rejects it; they still remain in perfect harmony as Christians, and merely
differ a little in opinion as philosophers. It is possible, according to this remarkable theory, to err to any
extent in philosophy, but not possible to err at all in
religion. One would have been glad to ask this Doctor
of Divinity, since that is his title, just for the sake of
information, how a false philosophy can possibly be a
true religion? But it is probable that he would have
declined to answer the question. A celebrated person
once said: "O Liberty, how many crimes are committed
in thy name." Perhaps, we may say in our turn: "O
Philosophy, how much nonsense is talked in thine."

I have detained you too long, though I have said
but little, and said that little imperfectly. Yet we
have seen, perhaps with sufficient evidence, this essen-

38

tial distinction between the kingdoms of Order and
Chaos, between the Church and the Sects; that in the
one everything reflects the presence and the attributes
of God, while in the other, man has usurped His place,
and reigns alone, surrounded by all the customary
emblems of human feebleness, vanity, and imperfection.
I must not conclude without calling your attention to
this correlative fact, that in the Church, which is God's
realm, effectual provision has been made for the remedy
of all transient disorders, and the prompt repair of all
waste and loss; while in the Sects, where man is the
sole lord, and must do his own work because there is
none to help him, no sign of any such provision exists.
This also is just the distinction which we might have
expected to find between what is human and what is
Divine.

Every student of nature has noted with admiration
the astonishing *faculty of recuperation* which it displays
in all its departments. The same phenomenon exists in
the kingdom of grace. In both a machinery has been
created, and is constantly in active operation, by which
wounded and enfeebled organisms are able to attain a
new vitality. I ask your permission to dwell for an
instant on this analogy. It was worthy of our God so
to arrange the order of the universe, and assure its
stability, that no fatal shock, no irreparable disaster,
should be permitted to disturb its equilibrium. The
sun may not quit its allotted place, nor the planets
wander from their appointed sphere. In like manner,
though her habitual lot is trial and suffering, the
Church remains for ever unmoved on her eternal foundations. But if God has thus limited the field beyond
which no serious derangement of His work shall be
allowed, either in the world of nature or of grace, till
the end of time, His Providence has not excluded the

possibility of disorders on a smaller scale. Yet even
in tolerating these apparent defects, He only gives a
new proof of His omnipotence. Both in the material
and the spiritual creation, there resides a marvellous
power of correcting momentary disorders, of applying
a remedy to transient corruptions. With respect to
the first, you know that there is no more elementary
truth in physics than that life is actually begotten of
death. You see this every day in the vegetable world,
and even in the animal economy, you are not ignorant
by what process the daily waste of tissues and other
parts is incessantly supplied, and that even the most
formidable ravages of disease in the human frame can
be repaired by that astonishing growth of matter which
is called the granulation of new flesh. I wish you to
observe, without attempting to multiply such examples,
that these phenomena of reproduction, which you notice
with so much admiration in the kingdom of matter, are
incomparably more beautiful and surprising in the
kingdom of grace, and that they exist, as I said, only
in the Catholic. Church.

In the kingdom of souls there are two possible evils,
— corruption of doctrine, and corruption of morals.
For both, God has provided remedies so divinely effi-
cacious, that nothing which occurs in the material universe can be fitly compared with them, except by way
of analogy. Thus, in the sphere of morals, there resides in the Church a power of healing so mighty, that
only the direct co-operation of God can explain its ac-
tion. No depravity, however inveterate, can resist it.
I need only remind you that St. Mary Magdalen and
St. Mary of Egypt, are both canonized Saints, whom
the Church has raised upon her altars as models of
humanity. Tens of thousands since their day, who
have fallen as they fell, have been *created anew* as they

were, by the omnipotence of the same remedial Sacraments. It would not become me to attempt to describe them. Such a theme is too high for me. I leave it to those who speak with consecrated lips. But I ask, and you have already anticipated the question, what similar provision for sick souls exists outside the Church of God?

My personal experience, as one whose misfortune it was to be during seven years a teacher in the Temple of Chaos, compels me to affirm that there is *none*. According to my observation, the common case of those who sin mortally outside the Church is this, that when the hour of awakening arrives, — for many it never comes at all, or only comes too late,—they either embrace some new heresy still more monstrous than any which they had previously professed, or fall into deadly presumption. I remember being called, during the melancholy period of my life to which I have alluded, to the death-bed of a woman in whom it was impossible to detect a single feature of the Christian character.. Yet she replied to my exhortation, with the sneer of pride on her dying lips: "You need not trouble yourself about me, Sir, I was saved long ago." In this case, as in many like it, I was reminded of the malediction pronounced upon those "whose last state is worse than the first." Nor was it more consoling to witness other deaths, in which counterfeit rites and spurious sacraments strove to hide the mortal wound of the soul without being able to heal it, and copied the external forms of the Christian ritual only to disguise the ruin which they were powerless to avert. But I pass from this sorrowful subject to the corruption of doctrine.

To record all that the Church has done from the beginning to preserve the faith from corruption would be to write her history. You know how in every age, she alone has baffled all the arts of the wicked one, and preserved the deposit entrusted to her keeping. I will not remind you of her victories over every heresy in ages gone by, but will ask you to notice only a single example in our own time. It will amply suffice as an illustration of the point which we are considering. It so happens that during the present generation four of the most eminent of her priests, conspicuous by the splendour of their intellectual gifts, have merited the admonition or provoked the censures of the Church. We need not hesitate to recall the fact, for it will be found only to add new lustre to her imperishable glory. De Lamennais and Gioberti, Rosmini and Ventura,— of whom the two last have been imitators of the lowly Fénelon, the two first of the arrogant Tertullian,—are examples in our own day of the ceaseless vigilance of the successors of St. Peter, in rebuking and destroying error. The two first resisted him, and withered away like a tree blasted by lightning ; the two last obeyed his paternal remonstrance, and by their humility acquired fresh titles to the love and respects of Christians, to whom they have bequeathed so excellent an example. Such is the sleepless fidelity of God's Vicar, and such are the fruits of his Divine mission to preserve the children entrusted to him in the purity and simplicity of our most holy faith. Before his presence error hides her face, and the spirits of darkness, despairing of success, return to the abyss from which they came out.

And how is it with the Sects? Far from warring against religious error, they exist only to maintain and defend its sovereign rights! They claim to *believe* whatever their own diseased imagination may persuade them to accept, and to *teach* whatever the "itching ears" of others may induce them to hear. What is feebly repudiated by one sect is cordially welcomed by another,

6

and even in the same sect every conflicting interpretation of revealed truth has exactly the same title to respect, because it has its origin in the same right of private judgment, and appeals to the same personal infallibility in those to whom it is addressed. The Church of England, the most powerful of all Protestant communities, by reason of her vast endowments and connection with the State, differs from the other sects mainly in this, that within her fold are taught at the same time *all* the errors maintained in every other, in addition to those which have been invented by herself. And they are all taught with equal authority, and with the same absolute immunity from remonstrance or correction. How should one man remonstrate with another for doing what he claims the right to do himself, or correct in his neighbour the aberrations which he may adopt as his own whenever he feels inclined to do so? And thus the eternal confusion of the Kingdom of Chaos is renewed from generation to generation, as one wave follows another in a stormy and tumultuous sea, and while the Church reflects in every age the unbroken Unity of God, the Sects represent only the strife and disorder which is the eternal portion of the fallen spirits in their own home, and which they have succeeded too well in introducing into ours, wherever they are not confronted by those invincible allies, the Mother of God and the Vicar of Christ.

It is a satisfaction to me, and will be at least an equal satisfaction to you, that I have now arrived at the last point upon which I think it necessary to trouble you with a few words. We have compared the Temples of Order and Chaos, as carefully as the time at our disposal permitted, in some of their most conspicuous features. It remains only to determine, as far as we have the means of doing so, what will be the relative position of the worshippers in each, when both temples shall have ceased to exist in their present form. Without this final enquiry, all that we have already said would be incomplete.

With respect to Catholics, it is evident that, in passing from the Church on earth to the Church in heaven, no change need come upon *them*, except that which is implied in passing from the state of grace to the state of glory. They will be *one* there, as they have been one here. For *them* the miracle of supernatural Unity is already worked. That mark of God's Hand is already upon them. That sign of God's election is already graven upon their foreheads. Faith indeed will be replaced by sight, but this will be no real change, because what they *see* in the next world will be what they have *believed* in this. The same *Sacramental King*, to borrow an expression of Father Faber, whom here they have worshipped upon the Altar, will there be their everlasting portion. The same gracious Madonna, who has so often consoled them in the trials of this life, will introduce her own children to the glories of the next. They will not in that hour have to "buy oil" for *their* lamps, for they are already kindled at the lamp of the sanctuary. No wedding-robe will have to be provided for *them*, for they received it long ago at the baptismal font, and have washed away its stains in the tribunal of penance. The faces of the Saints and Angels will not be strange to *them*, for have they not been familiar with them from infancy as friends, companions, and benefactors? And being thus, even in this world, of the household of faith, and the family of God, not only no shadow of change need pass upon *them*, but to vary in one iota from what they now believe and practice would simply cut them off from the Communion of Saints, and be the most overwhelming disaster which could befal them.

It is evident, on the other hand, that if the children of Chaos are to enter heaven,—a lot which we earnestly desire for them,—*they* can only do so after undergoing a radical and fundamental change. This, I say, is evident, for this reason among others, because *they* are *not one*, and nothing is more indisputably certain than this, that there can be no division in heaven. "God is not the God of dissension," says St. Paul, "but of peace," and if He has not suffered any interruption of Unity even in the Church Militant, the most disordered imagination cannot suppose the He will tolerate it in the Church Triumphant. How should disunion exist in the very presence of God? It would not be more monstrous to suppose that sin could sit on His right hand, throned and crowned. It follows, that if the members of the rival sects, which make up in their aggregate the great army of Chaos, are to enter heaven, whatever else they may take in with them, they must leave their differences at the door. Heaven is not a debating society, in which the disputes and contradictions of the children of error are to be eternally perpetuated. They have had *their* reign on earth, but must not expect to continue it in heaven. *There* dwells absolute and eternal Unity, the Unity of the Undivided Godhead, the same Unity which in the Catholic Church has already triumphed even over the frailties of men, and which, as far as *Catholics* are concerned, will only be renewed and perfected in the company of the elect.

If, indeed, it were possible,—and with this observation I conclude,—that the children of the Sects should enter heaven in their present state, each with his own personal creed, his own particular corruption of Christianity, have you ever considered what must be the inevitable result? We are told that there are in heaven, besides Angels and Archangels, Thrones, Dominions, Principalities, and Powers. Imagine, then, if you can, an Episcopalian Archangel leaning over the battlements of heaven in hot dispute with a Methodist Seraph, or an angry Presbyterian Throne flinging texts of Scripture in the face of a Baptist Principality. What a heaven it would be! Who can conceive the consternation of the Angels in having such a company thrust upon them? Farewell, for ever, the peace which they have known from the first hour of their creation. Chaos has mounted up into heaven, and Order unfolds her wings to fly from an abode where she has no longer a home. I do not affirm that no Episcopalian, Methodist, or Presbyterian will enter heaven, but only that before they do so, since God will certainly remain what *He* is, *they* must cease to be what they are, and become something which now they are not. From this dilemma they can escape only by supposing,—and perhaps we shall some day see a new sect of which this will be the distinctive tenet,—that each denomination will have a heaven to itself, and that the inhabitants of one heaven will not be permitted to visit those of another, for fear they should renew in the next world the quarrels which were their chief employment in this. Well, this arrangement has perhaps the merit of simplicity, but it wants something to make it complete. Will the children of Chaos tell us, if they can, in which of these earth-begotten heavens where neither Saint nor Angel would stoop to dwell, will the Holy and Undivided One establish His throne?